My Little Book of
Frogs and Toads

By Patricia Relf
Illustrated by Rosiland Solomon

Kathy Carlstead, Ph.D., Research Associate, National Zoological Park,

Smithsonian Institution, Consultant

A GOLDEN BOOK • NEW YORK
Western Publishing Company, Inc., Racine, Wisconsin 53404

What Are Frogs and Toads?

Frogs and toads are small animals. When they are young, they have to live in water, like fish, in order to breathe and move. As they grow, their bodies change so that they can breathe air and move about on land. Because they start out in water but can later live on land, frogs and toads are called *amphibians*, which means "living two lives."

Which Is Which?

Frogs and toads come in many shapes, colors, and sizes. There are more than three thousand different kinds in the world. It is not always easy to tell frogs from toads. Frogs usually have moist skin and long, strong back legs that help them jump. They live in or near water.

snout

tongue

ear

Leopard frog

Toads usually have dry skin and are covered with bumps that people call warts. Most toads have short back legs, and they walk or hop rather than jump. Adult toads usually live on land.

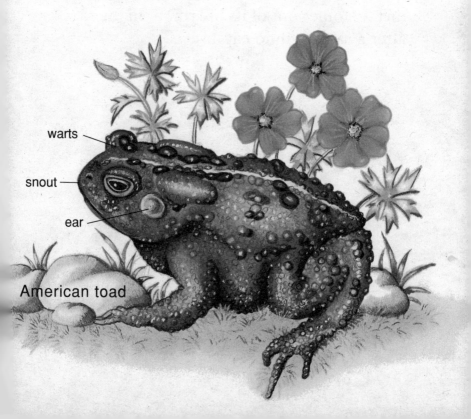

warts

snout

ear

American toad

Home, Sweet Home

Frogs and toads can live in all kinds of places. The spadefoot toad lives in a burrow, or hole, underground. Using its back feet as shovels, it digs down and backward into the dirt. It comes out of its burrow at night or after a rainstorm to eat insects.

Treefrog

Green frog

Treefrogs live in trees and on other plants. The ends of their toes are flat and sticky to help them cling to branches and leaves.

Green frogs live in ponds and swamps. They eat crayfish and insects. The male's throat is often a yellowish color.

Babies

Most frogs and toads lay their eggs in water. Some lay thousands of eggs at a time.

Tadpoles, which look like tiny fish, hatch from the eggs. They live in water, eating small plants. Like fish, tadpoles have gills to help them breathe underwater.

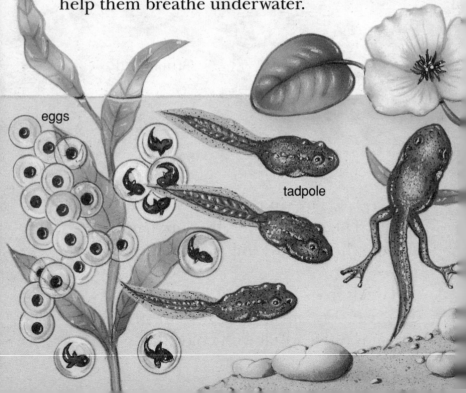

eggs

tadpole

As tadpoles get bigger, they grow legs, develop lungs, and lose their tails.

A few weeks after hatching, the tadpoles have changed into small frogs or toads. Now they can live on land, breathing air.

Unusual Frog Parents

The mother marsupial frog does not lay her eggs in a pond or river. Instead, she carries them in a special pouch on her back. There, twenty or more eggs hatch into tadpoles and grow. When they have legs and can live on land, the tiny frogs hop out of their mother's pouch.

The eggs of Darwin's frogs are cared for by the father. After the female lays the eggs, the male scoops them up with his tongue and slides them into his vocal pouch, the large area in his throat that he usually uses for making sounds. The eggs hatch and grow into tadpoles. When they are big enough, the father spits them out!

A Great Swimmer

The orange mantella frog is tiny—
only one inch long—but it is a strong
swimmer. Its webbed feet push against the
water like paddles. It eats ants and small
insects that it finds on plants and trees.

A "See-Through" Frog

Glass frogs are not made of glass, but you can see through their skin. You can see the veins, bones, heart, and other parts inside the frog's body. Glass frogs live in Central and South America.

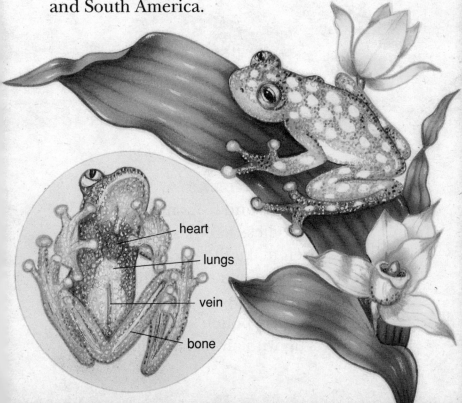

heart

lungs

vein

bone

Noisemakers

Most male toads and frogs make noises, from peeps and clicks to croaks and growls. The males often make these sounds to attract females, but they sometimes use them to warn other males to stay away.

The male's vocal pouch, just below the mouth, puffs up with air like a balloon.

mouth

vocal pouch

vocal cords

lungs

When the air flows back and forth between the vocal pouch and the lungs, it passes over the vocal cords. The vocal cords begin to move and make sounds.

When bullfrogs croak, it sounds as if they are saying, "Jug o' rum."

Great Plains toads sing with lots of loud, low notes during rainstorms.

Dinnertime

Most toads and frogs eat insects. A frog or toad flicks out its sticky tongue and, lightning fast, wraps it around a flying insect. Larger toads and frogs may also eat mice, lizards, and even other frogs. They use their front feet to stuff food into their mouth.

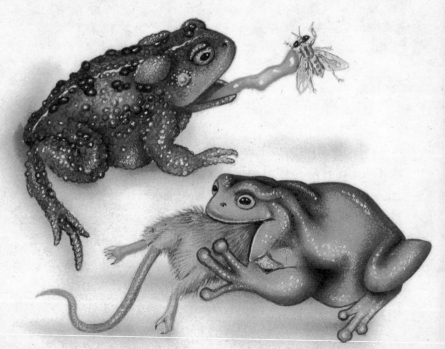

Helpful Giant

The giant toad, also known as the marine toad, can grow to be more than nine inches long—about as long as a lady's shoe. Farmers welcome this toad because it eats insects that harm the crops. When it is in danger, it can squirt poison from glands behind its ears.

Self-Defense

Frogs and toads have many ways to protect themselves against larger animals.

The Asiatic horned frog can hide itself on the forest floor because it looks just like a leaf.

The canyon treefrog changes its skin color to match the nearby background.

Poison dart frogs are the most poisonous of all frogs and toads. Their bright colors warn other animals that they are not good to eat.

Graceful Glider

The flying frog lives in the treetops of the Malayan jungle. It can't fly like a bird, but it jumps long distances, using its webbed feet to glide and steer itself through the air.

When Winter Comes

In places where winters are cold, frogs and toads hibernate, or sleep through the winter. Frogs can sleep in the mud, even underwater, breathing through their skin. Toads find a protected place under a log or rock. In the spring, both frogs and toads come out of hibernation to mate.

Backyard Friends

Most toads don't wander far from their homes except to mate. You may find the same toad in your yard or a park for many years. The skin of some toads gives off a substance that can make your skin sore, so be sure to wash your hands soon after you handle a toad.

Largest and Smallest

The largest toad is the marine, or giant, toad. The largest marine toad ever seen was fifteen inches long and weighed almost six pounds.

The smallest frog is the Cuban frog. It is less than half an inch long—about the size of a dime!

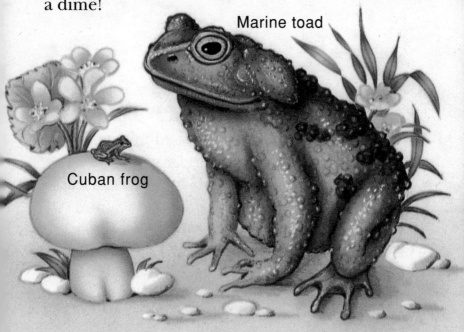

Marine toad

Cuban frog

Frogs, Toads, and People

Why are people so interested in frogs and toads? These amazing animals are fun to watch. They also eat insects that carry diseases or harm farm crops. By studying frogs and toads, scientists can learn more about ponds, rivers, and the rest of the world around us. Water and land that are safe for frogs and toads are probably safe for people, too.